THREE POETS
TRES POETAS

THREE POETS
TRES POETAS

Marlena Maduro Baraf
Carmen Bardeguez-Brown
Julio César Paz

MARROWSTONE PRESS

Copyright © 2022 by Marlena Maduro Baraf with respect to the following poems: "Tiritit Pritpit," "The Net," "I Live Inside," "In a city," and "Apricot."

Copyright © 2022 by Carmen Bardeguez-Brown with respect to the following poems: "The New Normal Rant," "On My Way to Paradiso," "Timbales, Maracas y Trompetas," "Some day," and "Ode to My New Home."

Copyright © 2022 by Julio César Paz with respect to the following poems: "Before the Storm," "Juggler's Magic," "A Fish Market in the Rain," and "A Blackout on a Mild October Evening."

Copyright © 2022 by Marlena Maduro Baraf, Carmen Bardeguez-Brown, and Julio César Paz with respect to all other material

All Rights Reserved

ISBN: 978-0-578-37310-2

Cover art by Chang Lek © 2021
Book design by Marrowstone Design

...la poesía es como el pan, de todos
—Roque Dalton, "Como tú"

Buenos días/Buenas noches

We found each other across enormous distances of time and space—three Latino poets—sharing our love of words, music, and stories, supporting one another, talking poetry. In spite of different life experiences in our native countries, we discovered quickly that we had much in common, and it starts with language and with being Latino. We gave with an open heart.

Carmen, Puertoriqueña and Nuyorican, in Thailand; Marlena, Panameña, in the United States, and Julio César, Cubano, in Vietnam. We met on computer screens in time zones 12 hours apart. The world was in chaos. Our commitment to write and learn from one another helped us navigate the transformations initiated by the Pandemic of 2020.

Marlena Maduro Baraf
Carmen Bardeguez-Brown
Julio César Paz

Marlena Maduro Baraf

Apricot is not the color she wore

Marlena Maduro Baraf is a master of the art of concision. With words hand picked out of a carefully grown garden, she finds a way to make her poems dance on the page. Such a musicality invites varied readings of her poems, making us accomplices in the creative process. She appeals to the child who lives in each one of us with lines that seem incidental but, like Lorca's duende, are indispensable. Marlena takes us by the hand and invites us to discover the beauty we pass by as we busily walk our own paths.

Julio César, Hanoi.

Tiritit Pritpit

                high trills
        triple
        trills
      high octane
undertone
on the left
        a nasal wing over there
    the woodpecker's

            rat-tat-tat

The Net

Fishing for fish (not to keep)
                    with a net
The sunfish got trapped in the net

My granddaughter
felt the sunfish's distress
    Call dad
    Call dad
    Call dad!

Her heart is beating as fast
   as the sunfish's heart
Do fish have hearts

              and circulation?
         Why don't I know this?

I Live Inside

Yes, I live inside the flower
but there is no need for you
to come and visit me

That's it.
I live inside the flower

No! Let me be.
I live inside the flower
and you don't fit

Yes. I laugh inside your hand
Can you even hear me?

Pandemonium
No. 6 feet apart
Stay—6 feet apart
But let us love lavishly
Till death do us part

/ after Katerina Rudcenkova

In a city

                        even
under assault by an enemy
virus the girl at Pi bakery on Broome waits
when I linger over little rolls of baklava
with pistachios take your time   my
husband's hot chocolate with skim
    and smiles as I fumble
                        Manhattan
is a town of small islands
      contrary to false thoughts
and the woman in stacked black
boots with her honey yellow hair packed
on her head   with a clip
winks at me   before calling on her cellphone
all tongue and lips – Russian and red
alligator satchel
                       Like cockroaches
when apartment dwellers disappear
on holiday we're inside out   Where
are the children?
    and the Spanish woman on Mulberry
      whose voice dances
         and everyone

I asked my husband
who he'd choose to spend one day with
    you set the conditions
He imagined his father
who might not
recognize him would not
    understand
I choose my grandmother
      who she was – who I was

Apricot

Ap-ri-cot three syllables with that juicy "pree" sound in
English ending with a lilting, cutting consonant.
In Spanish it's *albaricoque* and just as delicious, a short
tapatéo flamenco
on the wooden table.

    Ahl-bah-ree-kok-keh.   Say it.

But apricot is not the color she wore.
I must save apricot for a poem where I am not
cornered into speaking ordinary truths.

Carmen Bardeguez-Brown

Some day but not yet

Carmen Bardeguez-Brown's poems are a lesson in history. Her poems contain an irrepressible musicality that describes a whole lifetime—ending with the current moment: zip codes, zip codes, zip codes.

Resistance, daring, joy, deep Caribbean rhythms—these are the words I would choose to describe the sources of her talent. I am in awe of Carmen's courage to sing and be in the world.

Marlena, New York.

The New Normal Rant

Chirping birds
Crumbs
empty spaces
silence
Kids playing
People dying
Masks
Mandates
Jobs gone
Thai greeting
No hugs.
Breathe
Hiroshima without a bomb
Orwellian language out of control
Numbers
Numbers
All those numbers
scary emails
You are on your own
Numbers
Numbers
Faceless numbers
Every
single
day.
Breathe
Impermanence
Mandates
Sirens
Mandates
The Apex
Mandates
Flattening the curve
Mandates

Common burials
Social Distancing
Vaccination
Pharmaceuticals exoneration
Wuhan lab
NIH
CDC
World Health Organization
Complicit
wash your hands
stay home
Pause
Repeat
wash your hands
Stay home
Pause
Repeat
trust the government
trust your instincts.
Breathe
Trust Rin Tin Tin and the cartoon world
While they kill prophets all over the world
Malcolm X, Dr. King, JFK, blown away in front of TV
Medgar Evers & Albizu, & Lumumba all had a vision
Poison blankets are now given to all
The best minds of my generation destroyed
Lies & madness postcards tragedy
Cuba's embargo is a real crime, you know
Puerto Rican colonial status burning the island from side to side
Bang-Bang-Bang
Keep sipping amnesia
clicking smartphones
suicide selfies
silent killing is in cruise control
Keep listening to the lyrics of Armageddon
Your body is consumed by fear & spiritual starvation
Wars and war are the permanent crack fix to those above and the minions in between

Korea
Vietnam
Iraq
Afghanistan
It is already cashed in the bank
Covert invasions
International political assassinations
people dying of hopelessness & desperation
&
On January 6, Three Kings Day
Chickens running to roost their misguided anger on the fake American way
Breathe
Tuskegee
La Operación
Eisenhower last words
9 million die of Hunger
Is there a vaccine for that?
Fascist Meta Verse
Racism & Genocide
Technologically lobotomized.
Now what?
Breathe
Now what?
Breathe

On My Way to Paradiso

I left behind the smell of sea salt,
The sweetness of guayaba and the crimson beauty of the amapola.
A pink paper mache note was sewn on my right arm with Mami's last lullabies & I covered it with warm kisses.
I see purple mountains & black holes gulping down nebulas pregnant with life.
A green meadow suddenly re-appears covered with velvety red broken hearts.
I walk past half baked dreams & see
Broken bones scatter
burning in flames
Am I on my way to Heaven?
Crystalline water bathe my dry skin & I open my mouth
   & drink
Ancient stars dance with fireflies
   & sing melodies that I don't understand
I am tired &
I murmur a prayer
in English as my Spanish hangs in a dusty closet.
No turning back
Scorched white magnolias
   & a broken compass
Will I, feel the embraces of my loved ones, again?
I left my old self searching for answers
& walk into the unknown
& I'm quietly birthing into my own.

Tim   Maracas   Trompetas
　　Bales　　　　Y

Beauty
Is
In
The eyes of the beholder.
Pelo
　　Malo
Que se cree esa prieta
Mira Goya beans
　　　　　Who do you think you are?
Pelo
　　Malo
You
　　Are
Pretty
　　For
Your
Kind.
Flatten the curve
Wear a mask.
I can't breathe.
9 minutes & 29 seconds
I CAN'T BREATHE. I CAN'T BREATHE.
I CAN'T BREATHE. I CAN'T BREATHE.
I CAN'T BREATHE. I CAN'T BREATHE. I CAN'T BREATHE. I CAN'T BREATHE. I CAN'T BREATHE. I CAN'T BREATHE.
Another
　　　Black Man
Killed

Intubation
Incarceration
Which Pandemic are we dealing with?
The zip codes
The zip codes
 The
 Zip
Codes.

Some day

Someday I will
Let my gray hair define my moments
But not yet
Loud laughs
revel
in the tightness of dry tears
A stout body
An Atlas of pain & resistance.

My son & daughter in law called me
"La mama"
My brown hands have a few callouses & I just saw a varicose vein on my right leg.

I witness Palos Verdes blue light butterflies die as they barely come out from their cocoon.

Some day
Maroon wisdom songs will console me as
  I sing
Shackle free
& the shadows will disappear.

Someday
But not yet
Some
day
I will.

Ode to My New Home

I'm ok. I'm ok.
Chiangmai is my new home, now.
Do you understand?
I miss my family. I miss New York.
I am living, now in Thailand.

ฉันสบายอี ฉันสบยดี
ฉันอาค้ยอยู่ที่ เชียงใหม่ ตอนนี
คณข้ใจไหม?
คิดถึ้งนะ ครอบค้รว
ฉัน อค้ยอย่ ราชอาณาจ้รไทย.

Julio César Paz

Feet flat nap

The poetry of Julio César Paz is an invitation to navigate surreal worlds of emotions rooted in life. Through the lens of his Caribbean experience we feel the sadness for what was left behind and the excitement of what is possible. Julio César uses words to paint a landscape of contrite emotions in order to play tricks on the sadness of the present reality.

Carmen, Chiang Mai.

Before the Storm

I could forget
but
the insane tendency of your lips
biting the sand
at dawn before the rain

it was just
the beach and
your cold-blooded
lips

on my neck
announcing
a new storm.

Juggler's Magic

Sitting at the airport
like a luggage not claimed
going in circles
wait for   stamps,
fold my bones
carefully to fit
inside the carry-on   pinkish, this time
juggler's magic
but the officer insists   frowns, daring
on sampling my spine
for future   cloning

monkeys

A Fish Market in the Rain

And then I saw them
left alone with the last passing bikes
tilting their tongues to secure a couple of raindrops

the sun crawling   the shrugged houses
like the open beaks of *chim lac*
the roof slates mirroring the heat
the lines on their necks where their grandchildren could probably
play hopscotch.
But no one else was there
just the lines and the mud crabs
the sun-harnessed stares
and hand fans busily piling mounds of fish scales.

These grandmothers and những cái mẹt
     feet flat squat
bamboo baskets on the curb
     feet flat hack
swaying bulging eyes
     feet flat nap
     feet flat chat

they sell kneeling dreams
     vegetables & fish
and a smiling talk for some tip
          or time.

No one buys in the damp hour,
the boys on the bikes rush under their áo mưa and forget
              their mothers.

A Blackout on a Mild October Evening

The children play under the
threshold of dust,
gentle,
disturbing the dream of the curtains
awakening the shadows of the barefoot
                              mirrors.
And their mothers, in the lonely night,
knit their bones into yet
another winter stocking.

Marlena Maduro Baraf—editor, essayist, poet—immigrated to the United States from her native Panama and is author of the memoir, *At the Narrow Waist of the World*. Her essays, stories and poems have been published in Ms. Magazine, Lilith, Sweet Lit, Huffpost, the Ekphrastic Review, Night Heron Barks, On the Seawall, Poets Reading the News, and elsewhere. Marlena's blog, *Soy/Somos, I Am/We Are*, features conversations with Latinos living in the USA. She can be reached at www.marlenamadurobaraf.com

Carmen Bardeguez-Brown is a Puerto Rican-Nuyorican poet. Her work has been published in magazines and anthologies such as: Tribes, Phatitude Cultural Magazine, Nuyorican Poets Writers Vol.1 edited by Dr. Nancy Mercado, Xanath Caraza Poetry Blog, On the Seawall, Aloud: Voices of the Nuyorican Poets Café, Manteca: An Anthology of Afro-Latino Poets and many more. She has read her work at The Nuyorican Poets Café, The Fez, Mad Alex Foundation, Smoke, The Soho Arts Festival, Long wood Gallery, The Kitchen, The Bowery Poetry club, The Boricua College Poetry Series, Governor Island poetry Festival, Harvard University, Bronx Music Heritage Center, Greenlight Bookstore, Se Buscan Poetas Poetry reading series, Café Fuerte Reading Series and many other venues. Ms. Bardeguez-Brown is part of the exhibit Homenaje curated by Ricardo Muniz. The exhibit showcases 50 Puerto Ricans that have contributed to the heritage and culture of Puerto Ricans in New York City. The exhibit is at the permanent collection of Centro of Puerto Rican Studies @ Hunter College. She can be reached at cbbpoetry.wordpress.com

Julio César Paz is a Cuban-born poet and educator, raised in a small city by the sea. He lives in Hanoi where he shares his love of poetry through regular workshops with his students. He finds joy and inspiration in taking slow motion walks with his pet after school. He has co-authored *Lo que aprendi al otro lado del mundo* with Nuyorican poet Carmen Bardeguez Brown. His most recent collection is *Trinculo's Handwritings*. Find him on Twitter @JCPaz15

www.ingramcontent.com/pod-product-compliance
Lightning Source LLC
Chambersburg PA
CBHW032019290426
44109CB00013B/717